D0205317

Also by Paul Muldoon

New Weather (1973)

Mules (1977)

Why Brownlee Left (1980)

Quoof (1983)

Meeting the British (1987)

Selected Poems 1968–1986 (1987)

Madoc: A Mystery (1991)

The Faber Book of Contemporary Irish Poetry

(editor, 1986)

The Annals of Chile

THE ANNALS
OF CHILE

PAUL
MULDOON

Farrar, Straus and Giroux

New York

Copyright © 1994 by Paul Muldoon
All rights reserved
Published in Canada by HarperCollinsCanadaLtd
Published in the United Kingdom by Faber and Faber Limited, London
Printed in the United States of America
First published in 1994 by Farrar, Straus and Giroux

First Farrar, Straus and Giroux paperback edition, 1995

Library of Congress Cataloging-in-Publication Data
Muldoon, Paul.
The annals of Chile / Paul Muldoon.—1st ed.
p.   cm.
Poems.
I. Title.
PR6063.U367A84   1995   821'.914—dc20   94-10874   CIP

Acknowledgements are due to the editors of The American Poetry
Review, The Guardian, The Honest Ulsterman, The Independent on
Sunday, The Irish Review, London Review of Books, Observer
Magazine, Ploughshares, Poetry Book Society Supplement, The
Princeton Eclectic, Soho Square, Times Literary Supplement; also to the
British Broadcasting Corporation.

'The Sonogram' also appeared in The Prince of the Quotidian (The
Gallery Press; Wake Forest University Press, 1994), while 'Incantata'
was published in a limited edition by The Graphic Studio, Dublin. The
translation from Ovid's Metamorphoses was commissioned by Michael
Hofmann and James Lasdun for their anthology, After Ovid.

ISBN 0-374-52456-4

Contents

In memory of Brigid Regan

(1920–1974)

Part One

Ovid: *Metamorphoses*

Book VI, Lines 313–81

All the more reason, then, that men and women
should go in fear of Leto, their vengeful, vindictive numen,
and worship the mother of Apollo and Artemis
all the more zealously. This last tale of the demise
of Niobe brought others to mind, inspiring no less zeal
among the storytellers. 'On the fertile soil
of Lycia,' one began, 'the peasants, too, would scorn
Leto and pay the price. Since these Lycians were low-born,
the remarkable story of what happened
is scarcely known, though I saw with my own eyes the pond
where the wonder took place. My father, being too frail
to travel far himself, had sent me on the trail
of a string of prime bullocks he'd turned out
in those distant parts. He'd given me a Lycian scout
whom I followed over the rich
pasture till we came on a lake in the midst of which
stood an ancient altar, its stones blackened
by many sacrificial fires, set in a quicken
of reeds. The scout stopped in his tracks and said in a quiet
voice, "Have mercy on us", and I echoed
him, "Have mercy". When I asked my guide
if this was a shrine to the Naiads or Faunus or some such god
he replied, "Not at all, son: no common hill-god or genius
presides over this place but the one whom Juno
sentenced to wander round and round,
never to set foot on solid ground;
the goddess who dwells
here was the one to whom even Delos
gave short shrift,

though Delos itself was totally adrift;
on that unstable island, braced between a palm and a gnarled
olive, she brought her twins into the world,
then, clasping them to her breast,
set off again with Juno in hot pursuit.
By the time she touched down in Lycia, the bailiwick
of the Chimera, she was completely whacked
from her long travail; the intense heat
had left her drained; her breast-milk had run out.
Just then she stumbled upon a fair-to-middling-sized pond
in which some locals were cutting osiers and bent
and sawgrass and sedge.
Leto knelt by the water's edge
and made to cup her hands. But these local yokels
shook their reaping-hooks and sickles
and wouldn't let her drink. 'Why,' she begged them, 'why
would you deny me what's not yours to deny
since water, along with air and light,
is held by all in common, as a common right?
It's not as if I'm about to throw
myself headlong into your pool. My throat's so dry
and my tongue so swollen I can barely utter
this simple request for a life-giving drink of water.
If not for mine, then for my children's sakes,
I implore you to let us slake
our thirsts.' At that moment, the twins stretched
out their little hands. Who could fail to be touched
by such entreaties? These begrudgers, though, were moved
only to renew their threats and foul oaths:
then, to add insult
to injury, they began to stomp about and stir up the silt
on the bottom of the pond, muddying the water
out of no motive other than sheer spite.

[4]

That was it: that was as much as the Titan's daughter
could take; 'Since you've shown,' she cried, 'no soft spot
for me, in this soft spot you'll always stay.'
And stay they have: now they love nothing more than to play
in water, giving themselves over to total
immersion or contentedly skimming the surface; they dawdle
on the bank only to dive back in; now, as ever,
they work themselves into a lather
over some imagined slight; since they continually curse
and swear their voices are hoarse
while their necks, in so far as there's anything between
their heads and shoulders, are goitred; with their yellow
paunches set off by backs of olive-green,
they go leaping about the bog-hole with their frog-fellows." '

Brazil

§

When my mother snapped open her flimsy parasol
it was Brazil: if not Brazil,

then Uruguay.
One nipple darkening her smock.

My shame-faced *Tantum Ergo*
struggling through thurified smoke.

§

Later that afternoon would find
me hunched over the font

as she rinsed my hair. Her towel-turban.
Her terrapin

comb scuttling under the faucet.
I stood there in my string vest

and shorts while she repeated, '*Champi* . . . ?
Champi . . . ? *Champi* . . . ?' Then,

that bracelet of shampoo
about the bone, her triumphant '*ChampiÑON*'.

§

If not Uruguay, then Ecuador:
it must be somewhere on or near the equator

given how water
plunged headlong into water

when she pulled the plug.
So much for the obliq-

uity of leaving *What a Boy Should Know*
under my pillow: now *vagina* and *vas*

deferens made a holy show
of themselves. 'There is inherent vice

in everything,' as O'Higgins
would proclaim: it was O'Higgins who duly

had the terms 'widdershins'
and 'deasil' expunged from the annals of Chile.

Oscar

§

Be that as it may, I'm wakened by the moans
not of the wind
nor the wood-demons

but Oscar MacOscair, as we call the hound
who's wangled himself
into our bed: 'Why?' 'Why not?'

He lies between us like an ancient quoof
with a snout of perished gutta-
percha, and whines at something on the roof.

§

I'm suddenly mesmerized
by what I saw only today: a pair of high heels
abandoned on the road to Amherst.

§

And I've taken off, over the towns of Keady
and Aughnacloy and Caledon –
Et in Arcadia –

to a grave lit by acetylene
in which, though she preceded him
by a good ten years, my mother's skeleton

has managed to worm
its way back on top of the old man's,
and she once again has him under her thumb.

Milkweed and Monarch

§

As he knelt by the grave of his mother and father
the taste of dill, or tarragon –
he could barely tell one from the other –

filled his mouth. It seemed as if he might smother.
Why should he be stricken
with grief, not for his mother and father,

but a woman slinking from the fur of a sea-otter
in Portland, Maine, or, yes, Portland, Oregon –
he could barely tell one from the other –

and why should he now savour
the tang of her, her little pickled gherkin,
as he knelt by the grave of his mother and father?

§

He looked about. He remembered her palaver
on how both earth and sky would darken –
'You could barely tell one from the other' –

while the Monarch butterflies passed over
in their milkweed-hunger: 'A wing-beat, some reckon,
may trigger off the mother and father

of all storms, striking your Irish Cliffs of Moher
with the force of a hurricane.'
Then: 'Milkweed and Monarch "invented" each other.'

§

He looked about. Cow's-parsley in a samovar.
He'd mistaken his mother's name, 'Regan', for 'Anger':
as he knelt by the grave of his mother and father
he could barely tell one from the other.

Twice

It was so cold last night the water in the barrel grew a sod
of water: I asked Taggart and McAnespie to come over
and we sawed and sawed
for half an hour until, using a crowbar as a lever

in the way Archimedes always said
would shift the balance, we were somehow able to manoeuvre
out and, finally, stand on its side
in the snow that fifteen- or eighteen-inch thick manhole cover:

that 'manhole cover' was surely no more ice
than are McAnespie and Taggart still of this earth;
when I squinnied through it I saw 'Lefty' Clery, '*An Ciotach*',

grinning from both ends of the school photograph,
having jooked behind the three-deep rest of us to meet the
     Kodak's
leisurely pan; 'Two places at once, was it, or one place twice?'

Incantata

In memory of Mary Farl Powers

I thought of you tonight, *a leanbh*, lying there in your long
    barrow
colder and dumber than a fish by Francisco de Herrera,
as I X-Actoed from a spud the Inca
glyph for a mouth: thought of that first time I saw your pink
spotted torso, distant-near as a nautilus,
when you undid your portfolio, yes indeedy,
and held the print of what looked like a cankered potato
at arm's length – your arms being longer, it seemed, than
    Lugh's.

Even Lugh of the Long (sometimes the Silver) Arm
would have wanted some distance between himself and the
    army-worms
that so clouded the sky over St Cloud you'd have to seal
the doors and windows and steel
yourself against their nightmarish *déjeuner sur l'herbe*:
try as you might to run a foil
across their tracks, it was to no avail;
the army-worms shinnied down the stove-pipe on an
    army-worm rope.

I can hardly believe that, when we met, my idea of 'R and R'
was to get smashed, almost every night, on sickly-sweet
        Demarara
rum and Coke: as well as leaving you a grass widow
(remember how Krapp looks up 'viduity'?),
after eight or ten or twelve of those dark rums
it might be eight or ten or twelve o'clock before I'd land
back home in Landseer Street, deaf and blind
to the fact that not only was I all at sea, but in the doldrums.

Again and again you'd hold forth on your own version
        of Thomism,
your own *Summa*
Theologiae that in everything there is an order,
that the things of the world sing out in a great oratorio:
it was Thomism, though, tempered by *La Nausée*,
by His Nibs Sam Bethicket,
and by that Dublin thing, that an artist must walk down
        Baggott
Street wearing a hair-shirt under the shirt of Nessus.

'*D'éirigh me ar maidin*,' I sang, '*a tharraingt chun aoinigh
        mhóir*':
our first night, you just had to let slip that your secret amour
for a friend of mine was such
that you'd ended up lying with him in a ditch
under a bit of whin, or gorse, or furze,
somewhere on the border of Leitrim, perhaps, or Roscommon:
'gamine,' I wanted to say, 'kimono';
even then it was clear I'd never be at the centre of your
        universe.

Nor should I have been, since you were there already, your
        own *Ding*
an sich, no less likely to take wing
than the Christ you drew for a Christmas card as a pupa
in swaddling clothes: and how resolutely you would
        pooh pooh
the idea I shared with Vladimir and Estragon,
with whom I'd been having a couple of jars,
that this image of the Christ-child swaddled and laid in the
        manger
could be traced directly to those army-worm dragoons.

I thought of the night Vladimir was explaining to all and
        sundry
the difference between *geantrai* and *suantrai*
and you remarked on how you used to have a crush
on Burt Lancaster as Elmer Gantry, and Vladimir went to
        brush
the ash off his sleeve with a legerdemain
that meant only one thing – 'Why does he put up with this
        crap?' –
and you weighed in with 'To live in a dustbin, eating scrap,
seemed to Nagg and Nell a most eminent domain.'

How little you were exercised by those tiresome literary
        intrigues,
how you urged me to have no more truck
than the Thane of Calder
with a fourth estate that professes itself to be '*égalitaire*'
but wants only blood on the sand: yet, irony of ironies,
you were the one who, in the end,
got yourself up as a *retiarius* and, armed with net and trident,
marched from Mount Street to the Merrion Square arena.

[15]

In the end, you were the one who went forth to beard the lion,
you who took the DART line
every day from Jane's flat in Dun Laoghaire, or Dalkey,
dreaming your dream that the subterranean Dodder and Tolka
might again be heard above the *hoi polloi*
for whom Irish 'art' means a High Cross at Carndonagh or
    Corofin
and *The Book of Kells*: not until the lion cried craven
would the poor Tolka and the poor Dodder again sing out
    for joy.

I saw you again tonight, in your jump-suit, thin as a rake,
your hand moving in such a deliberate arc
as you ground a lithographic stone
that your hand and the stone blurred to one
and your face blurred into the face of your mother,
    Betty Wahl,
who took your failing, ink-stained hand
in her failing, ink-stained hand
and together you ground down that stone by sheer force of
    will.

I remember your pooh poohing, as we sat there on the
    'Enterprise',
my theory that if your name is Powers
you grow into it or, at least,
are less inclined to tremble before the likes of this bomb-blast
further up the track: I myself was shaking like a leaf
as we wondered whether the I.R.A. or the Red
Hand Commandos or even the Red
Brigades had brought us to a standstill worthy of Hamm
    and Clov.

Hamm and Clov; Nagg and Nell; Watt and Knott;
the fact is that we'd been at a standstill long before the night
things came to a head,
long before we'd sat for half the day in the sweltering heat
somewhere just south of Killnasaggart
and I let slip a name – her name – off my tongue
and you turned away (I see it now) the better to deliver
        the sting
in your own tail, to let slip your own little secret.

I thought of you again tonight, thin as a rake, as you bent
over the copper plate of 'Emblements',
its tidal wave of army-worms into which you all but
        disappeared:
I wanted to catch something of its spirit
and yours, to body out your disembodied *vox
clamantis in deserto*, to let this all-too-cumbersome device
of a potato-mouth in a potato-face
speak out, unencumbered, from its long, low, mould-filled
        box.

I wanted it to speak to what seems always true of the truly
        great,
that you had a winningly inaccurate
sense of your own worth, that you would second-guess
yourself too readily by far, that you would rally to any cause
before your own, mine even,
though you detected in me a tendency to put
on too much artificiality, both as man and poet,
which is why you called me 'Polyester' or 'Polyurethane'.

That last time in Dublin, I copied with a quill dipped in
    oak-gall
onto a sheet of vellum, or maybe a human caul,
a poem for *The Great Book of Ireland*: as I watched the low
swoop over the lawn today of a swallow
I thought of your animated talk of Camille Pissarro
and André Derain's *The Turning Road, L'Estaque*:
when I saw in that swallow's nest a face in a mud-pack
from that muddy road I was filled again with a profound
    sorrow.

You must have known already, as we moved from the
    'Hurly Burly'
to McDaid's or Riley's,
that something was amiss: I think you even mentioned a
    homeopath
as you showed off the great new acid-bath
in the Graphic Studio, and again undid your portfolio
to lay out your latest works; I try to imagine the strain
you must have been under, pretending to be as right as rain
while hearing the bells of a church from some long-flooded
    valley.

From the Quabbin reservoir, maybe, where the banks and
    bakeries
of a dozen little submerged Pompeii reliquaries
still do a roaring trade: as clearly as I saw your death-mask
in that swallow's nest, you must have heard the music
rise from the muddy ground between
your breasts as a nocturne, maybe, by John Field;
to think that you thought yourself so invulnerable, so
    inviolate,
that a little cancer could be beaten.

You must have known, as we walked through the ankle-deep
    clabber
with Katherine and Jean and the long-winded Quintus
    Calaber,
that cancer had already made such a breach
that you would almost surely perish:
you must have thought, as we walked through the woods
along the edge of the Quabbin,
that rather than let some doctor cut you open
you'd rely on infusions of hardock, hemlock, all the idle
    weeds.

I thought again of how art may be made, as it was by
    André Derain,
of nothing more than a turn
in the road where a swallow dips into the mire
or plucks a strand of bloody wool from a strand of barbed wire
in the aftermath of Chickamauga or Culloden
and builds from pain, from misery, from a deep-seated hurt,
a monument to the human heart
that shines like a golden dome among roofs rain-glazed
    and leaden.

I wanted the mouth in this potato-cut
to be heard far beyond the leaden, rain-glazed roofs of Quito,
to be heard all the way from the southern hemisphere
to Clontarf or Clondalkin, to wherever your sweet-severe
spirit might still find a toe-hold
in this world: it struck me then how you would be aghast
at the thought of my thinking you were some kind of ghost
who might still roam the earth in search of an earthly delight.

You'd be aghast at the idea of your spirit hanging over this vale
of tears like a jump-suited jump-jet whose vapour-trail
unravels a sky: for there's nothing, you'd say, nothing over
and above the sky itself, nothing but cloud-cover
reflected in a thousand lakes; it seems that Minne-
sota itself means 'sky-tinted water', that the sky is a great slab
of granite or iron ore that might at any moment slip
back into the worked-out sky-quarry, into the worked-out
    sky-mines.

To use the word 'might' is to betray you once too often,
    to betray
your notion that nothing's random, nothing arbitrary:
the gelignite weeps, the hands fly by on the alarm clock,
the 'Enterprise' goes clackety-clack
as they all must; even the car hijacked that morning in
    the Cross,
that was preordained, its owner spread on the bonnet
before being gagged and bound or bound
and gagged, that was fixed like the stars in the Southern Cross.

The fact that you were determined to cut yourself off in your
    prime
because it was *pre*-determined has my eyes abrim:
I crouch with Belacqua
and Lucky and Pozzo in the Acacacac-
ademy of Anthropopopometry, trying to make sense of the
    '*quaquaqua*'
of that potato-mouth; that mouth as prim
and proper as it's full of self-opprobrium,
with its '*quaquaqua*', with its 'Quoiquoiquoiquoiquoiquoi-
    quoiq'.

That's all that's left of the voice of Enrico Caruso
from all that's left of an opera-house somewhere in Matto
 Grosso,
all that's left of the hogweed and horehound and cuckoo-pint,
of the eighteen soldiers dead at Warrenpoint,
of the Black Church clique and the Graphic Studio claque,
of the many moons of glasses on a tray,
of the brewery-carts drawn by moon-booted drays,
of those jump-suits worn under your bottle-green worsted
 cloak.

Of the great big dishes of chicken lo mein and beef chow mein,
of what's mine is yours and what's yours mine,
of the oxlips and cowslips
on the banks of the Liffey at Leixlip
where the salmon breaks through the either/or neither/nor
 nether
reaches despite the temple-veil
of itself being rent and the penny left out overnight on the rail
is a sheet of copper when the mail-train has passed over.

Of the bride carried over the threshold, hey, only to alight
on the limestone slab of another threshold,
of the swarm, the cast,
the colt, the spew of bees hanging like a bottle of Lucozade
from a branch the groom must sever,
of Emily Post's ruling, in *Etiquette*,
on how best to deal with the butler being in cahoots
with the cook when they're both in cahoots with the chauffeur.

Of that poplar-flanked stretch of road between Leiden
and The Hague, of the road between Rathmullen and
        Ramelton,
where we looked so long and hard
for some trace of Spinoza or Amelia Earhart,
both of them going down with their engines on fire:
of the stretch of road somewhere near Urney
where Orpheus was again overwhelmed by that urge to turn
back and lost not only Eurydice but his steel-strung lyre.

Of the sparrows and finches in their bell of suet,
of the bitter-sweet
bottle of Calvados we felt obliged to open
somewhere near Falaise, so as to toast our new-found *copains*,
of the priest of the parish
who came enquiring about our 'status', of the hedge-clippers
I somehow had to hand, of him running like the clappers
up Landseer Street, of my subsequent self-reproach.

Of the remnants of Airey Neave, of the remnants of
        Mountbatten,
of the famous *andouilles*, of the famous *boudins*
noirs et blancs, of the barrel-vault
of the Cathedral at Rouen, of the flashlight, fat and roll of felt
on each of their sledges, of the music
of Joseph Beuys's pack of huskies, of that baldy little bugger
mushing them all the way from Berncastel through Bacarrat
to Belfast, his head stuck with honey and gold-leaf like
        a mosque.

Of Benjamin Britten's *Lachrymae*, with its gut-wrenching
    viola,
of Vivaldi's *Four Seasons*, of Frankie Valli's,
of Braque's great painting *The Shower of Rain*,
of the fizzy, lemon or sherbet-green *Ranus ranus*
plonked down in Trinity like a little Naugahyde pouffe,
of eighteen soldiers dead in Oriel,
of the weakness for a little fol-de-rol-de-rolly
suggested by the gap between the front teeth of the Wife
    of Bath.

Of *A Sunday Afternoon on the Island of La Grande Jatte*,
    of Seurat's
piling of tesserae upon tesserae
to give us a monkey arching its back
and the smoke arching out from a smoke-stack,
of Sunday afternoons in the Botanic Gardens, going with
    the flow
of the burghers of Sandy Row and Donegal
Pass and Andersonstown and Rathcoole,
of the army Landrover flaunt-flouncing by with its heavy
    furbelow.

Of Marlborough Park, of Notting Hill, of the Fitzroy Avenue
immortalized by Van 'His real name's Ivan'
Morrison, 'and him the dead spit
of Padraic Fiacc', of John Hewitt, the famous expat,
in whose memory they offer every year six of their best milch
    cows,
of the Bard of Ballymacarrett,
of every ungodly poet in his or her godly garret,
of Medhbh and Michael and Frank and Ciaran and 'wee'
    John Qughes.

[23]

Of the Belfast school, so called, of the school of hard knocks,
of your fervent eschewal of stockings and socks
as you set out to hunt down your foes
as implacably as the *tóraidheacht* through the Fews
of Redmond O'Hanlon, of how that 'd' and that 'c' aspirate
in *tóraidheacht* make it sound like a last gasp in an
    oxygen-tent,
of your refusal to open a vent
but to breathe in spirit of salt, the mordant salt-spirit.

Of how mordantly hydrochloric acid must have scored
    and scarred,
of the claim that boiled skirrets
can cure the spitting of blood, of that dank
flat somewhere off Morehampton Road, of the unbelievable
    stink
of valerian or feverfew simmering over a low heat,
of your sitting there, pale and gaunt,
with that great prescriber of boiled skirrets, Dr John
    Arbuthnot,
your face in a bowl of feverfew, a towel over your head.

Of the great roll of paper like a bolt of cloth
running out again and again like a road at the edge of a cliff,
of how you called a Red Admiral a Red
Admirable, of how you were never in the red
on either the first or the last
of the month, of your habit of loosing the drawstring of
    your purse
and finding one scrunched-up, obstreperous
note and smoothing it out and holding it up, pristine and
    pellucid.

Of how you spent your whole life with your back to the wall,
of your generosity when all the while
you yourself lived from hand
to mouth, of Joseph Beuys's pack of hounds
crying out from their felt and fat 'Atone, atone, atone',
of Watt remembering the '*Krak! Krek! Krik!*'
of those three frogs' karaoke
like the still, sad, *basso continuo* of the great quotidian.

Of a ground bass of sadness, yes, but also a sennet of hautboys
as the fat and felt hounds of Beuys O'Beuys
bayed at the moon over a caravan
in Dunmore East, I'm pretty sure it was, or Dungarvan:
of my guest appearance in your self-portrait not as a hidalgo
from a long line
of hidalgos but a hound-dog, a *leanbh*,
a dog that skulks in the background, a dog that skulks
        and stalks.

Of that self-portrait, of the self-portraits by Rembrandt van
        Rijn,
of all that's revelation, all that's rune,
of all that's composed, all composed of odds and ends,
of that daft urge to make amends
when it's far too late, too late even to make sense of the clutter
of false trails and reversed horseshoe tracks
and the aniseed we took it in turn to drag
across each other's scents, when only a fish is dumber
        and colder.

Of your avoidance of canned goods, in the main,
on account of the exceeeeeeeeeeeeeeeeedingly high risk of
    ptomaine,
of corned beef in particular being full of crap,
of your delight, so, in eating a banana as ceremoniously
    as Krapp
but flinging the skin over your shoulder like a thrush
flinging off a shell from which it's only just managed to disinter
a snail, like a stone-faced, twelfth-century
FitzKrapp eating his banana by the mellow, yellow light
    of a rush.

Of the 'Yes, let's go' spoken by Monsieur Tarragon,
of the early-ripening jardonelle, the tumorous jardon,
    the jargon
of jays, the jars
of tomato relish and the jars
of Victoria plums, absolutely *de rigueur* for a passable
    plum baba,
of the drawers full of balls of twine and butcher's string,
of Dire Straits playing 'The Sultans of Swing',
of the horse's hock suddenly erupting in those boils and
    buboes.

Of the Greek figurine of a pig, of the pig on a terracotta frieze,
of the sow dropping dead from some mysterious virus,
of your predilection for gammon
served with a sauce of coriander or cumin,
of the slippery elm, of the hornbeam or witch-, or even wych-,
hazel that's good for stopping a haemor-
rhage in mid-flow, of the merest of mere
hints of elderberry curing everything from sciatica to a stitch.

Of the decree *condemnator*, the decree *absolvitor*, the decree
     nisi,
of *Aosdána*, of *an chraobh cnuais*,
of the fields of buckwheat
taken over by garget, inkberry, scoke – all names for
     pokeweed –
of *Mother Courage*, of *Arturo Ui*,
of those Sunday mornings spent picking at sesame
noodles and all sorts and conditions of dim sum,
of tea and ham sandwiches in the Nesbitt Arms hotel in
     Ardara.

Of the day your father came to call, of your leaving your
     sick-room
in what can only have been a state of delirium,
of how you simply wouldn't relent
from your vision of a blind
watch-maker, of your fatal belief that fate
governs everything from the honey-rust of your father's
     terrier's
eyebrows to the horse that rusts and rears
in the furrow, of the furrows from which we can no more
     deviate

than they can from themselves, no more than the map of
     Europe
can be redrawn, than that Hermes might make a harp from
     his *harpe*,
than that we must live in a vale
of tears on the banks of the Lagan or the Foyle,
than that what we have is a done deal,
than that the Irish Hermes,
Lugh, might have leafed through his vast herbarium
for the leaf that had it within it, Mary, to anoint and anneal,

than that Lugh of the Long Arm might have found in the midst
     of *lus*
na leac or *lus na treatha* or *Frannc-lus*,
in the midst of eyebright, or speedwell, or tansy, an antidote,
than that this *Incantata*
might have you look up from your plate of copper or zinc
on which you've etched the row upon row
of army-worms, than that you might reach out, arrah,
and take in your ink-stained hands my own hands stained
     with ink.

The Sonogram

Only a few weeks ago, the sonogram of Jean's womb
resembled nothing so much
as a satellite-map of Ireland:

now the image
is so well-defined we can make out not only a hand
but a thumb;

on the road to Spiddal, a woman hitching a ride;
a gladiator in his net, passing judgement on the crowd.

Footling

This I don't believe: rather than take a header
off the groyne
and into the ground swell,
yea verily, the *ground swell* of life,

she shows instead her utter
disregard – part diffidence, but mostly scorn –
for what lies behind the great sea-wall
and what knocks away at the great sea-cliff;

though she's been in training all spring and summer
and swathed herself in fat
and Saran-

Wrap like an old-time Channel swimmer,
she's now got cold feet
and turned in on herself, the phantom 'a' in Cesarian.

The Birth

Seven o'clock. The seventh day of the seventh month of
    the year.
No sooner have I got myself up in lime-green scrubs,
a sterile cap and mask,
and taken my place at the head of the table

than the windlass-women ply their shears
and gralloch-grub
for a footling foot, then, warming to their task,
haul into the inestimable

realm of apple-blossoms and chanterelles and damsons
    and eel-spears
and foxes and the general hubbub
of inkies and jennets and Kickapoos with their lemniscs
or peekaboo-quiffs of Russian sable

and tallow-unctuous vernix, into the realm of the widgeon —
the 'whew' or 'yellow-poll', not the 'zuizin' — .

Dorothy Aoife Korelitz Muldoon: I watch through floods
    of tears
as they give her a quick rub-a-dub
and whisk
her off to the nursery, then check their staple-guns for staples.

César Vallejo: *Testimony*

I will die in Paris, on a day the rain's been coming down hard,
a day I can even now recall.
I will die in Paris – I try not to take this too much to heart –
on a Thursday, probably, in the Fall.

It'll be like today, a Thursday: a Thursday on which, as I make
and remake this poem, the very bones
in my forearms ache.
Never before, along the road, have I felt more alone.

César Vallejo is dead: everyone used to knock him about,
they'll say, though he'd done no harm;
they hit him hard with a rod

and, also, a length of rope; this will be borne out
by Thursdays, by the bones in his forearms,
by loneliness, by heavy rain, by the aforementioned roads.

Cows

for Dermot Seymour

§

Even as we speak, there's a smoker's cough
from behind the whitethorn hedge: we stop dead in our
    tracks;
a distant tingle of water into a trough.

§

In the past half-hour – since a cattle-truck
all but sent us shuffling off this mortal coil –
we've consoled ourselves with the dregs

of a bottle of Redbreast. Had Hawthorne been a Gael,
I insist, the scarlet 'A' on Hester Prynne
would have stood for 'Alcohol'.

§

This must be the same truck whose tail-lights burn
so dimly, as if caked with dirt,
three or four hundred yards along the boreen

(a diminutive form of the Gaelic *bóthar*, 'a road',
from *bó*, 'a cow', and *thar*
meaning, in this case, something like 'athwart',

[33]

'boreen' has entered English 'through the air'
despite the protestations of the O.E.D.):
why, though, should one tail-light flash and flare,

then flicker-fade
to an after-image of tourmaline
set in a dark part-jet, part-jasper or -jade?

§

That smoker's cough again: it triggers off from drumlin
to drumlin an emphysemantiphon
of cows. They hoist themselves on to their trampoline

and steady themselves and straight away divine
water in some far-flung spot
to which they then gravely incline. This is no Devon

cow-coterie, by the way, whey-faced, with Spode
hooves and horns: nor are they the metaphysicattle of Japan
that have merely to anticipate

scoring a bull's-eye and, lo, it happens;
these are earth-flesh, earth-blood, salt of the earth,
whose talismans are their own jaw-bones

buried under threshold and hearth.
For though they trace themselves to the kith and kine
that presided over the birth

of Christ (so carry their calves a full nine
months and boast liquorice
cachous on their tongues), they belong more to the line

that's tramped these cwms and corries
since Cuchulainn tramped Aoife.
Again the flash. Again the fade. However I might allegorize

some oscaraboscarabinary bevy
of cattle there's no getting round this cattle-truck,
one light on the blink, laden with what? Microwaves? Hi-fis?

§

Oscaraboscarabinary: a twin, entwined, a tree, a Tuareg;
a double dung-beetle; a plain
and simple hi-firing party; an off-the-back-of-a-lorry drogue?

Enough of Colette and Céline, Céline and Paul Celan:
enough of whether Nabokov
taught at Wellesley or Wesleyan.

Now let us talk of slaughter and the slain,
the helicopter gun-ship, the mighty Kalashnikov:
let's rest for a while in a place where a cow has lain.

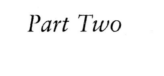

Part Two

Yarrow

Little by little it dawned on us that the row
of kale would shortly be overwhelmed by these pink
and cream blooms, that all of us

would be overwhelmed, that even if my da
were to lose an arm
or a leg to the fly-wheel

of a combine and be laid out on a tarp
in a pool of blood and oil
and my ma were to make one of her increasingly rare

appeals to some higher power, some *Deo*
this or that, all would be swept away by the stream
that fanned across the land.

All would be swept away: the altar where Montezuma's
daughter severed her own aorta
with an obsidian knife; where the young Ignatius

of Loyola knelt and, raising the visor of his bucket,
pledged himself either *Ad Major*
or *Ad Majorem Dei Gloriam*, I can't quite remember which.

For all would be swept away: the barn where the Pharaohs
had buried Tutankhamen;
where Aladdin found the magic lamp and ring;

where Ali Baba
watched the slave, Morgiana,
pour boiling oil on the thieves in their jars;

where Cicero smooth-talked the senators;
where I myself was caught up in the rush
of peers and paladins who ventured out with Charlemagne.

All would be swept away, all sold for scrap:
the hen-house improvised from a high-sided cattle-truck,
the coils of barbed wire, the coulter

of a plough, the pair of angle-iron
posts between which she'll waver, one day towards the end,
as she pins the clothes on the clothes-line.

For the moment, though, she thumbs through a seed-catalogue
she's borrowed from Tohill's of the Moy
while, quiet, almost craven,

he studies the grain in the shaft of a rake:
there are two palm-prints in blue stone
on the bib of his overalls

where he's absentmindedly put his hands
to his heart; in a den in St John's, Newfoundland, I browse
on a sprig of *Achillea millefolium*, as it's classed.

Achillea millefolium: with its bedraggled, feathery leaf
and pink (less red
than mauve) or off-white flower, its tight little knot

of a head,
it's like something keeping a secret
from itself, something on the tip of its own tongue.

Would that I might take comfort in the vestigial scent
of a yarrow-sprig, a yarrow-spurt
I've plucked from the somewhat unorthodox

funerary vase
that fills one grate:
from the other there's a chortle of methane-gas

(is it methane
that's so redolent of the apple-butt?)
through a snow-capped sierra of non-combustible coal.

Would that I might as readily follow
this nosegay of yarrow as Don Junipero Serra
led us all the way back

along *El Camino Real*
by the helter-skelter path
of poppies we'd sown in the sap-sweet April rain.

I zap the remote control: that same poor elk or eland
dragged down by a bobolink;
a Spanish *Lear*; the umpteenth *Broken Arrow*;

a boxing-match; Robert Hughes dismantling Dada;
a Michael Jackson video
in which our friends, the Sioux, will peel

the face off a white man whose metacarp-
al bones, with those of either talus,
they've already numbered; the atmosphere's so rare

that if Michael's moon-suit of aluminium foil
were suddenly to split at the seams
he'd not only buy, but fertilize, the farm.

Again and again I stare out across the fallow
where a herd of peccaries
(white-lipped musk-

pigs, as they're sometimes known) have beaten
a path through what was the cabbage-field
to where they wallow in whiskey and *bainne clabair*.

Again and again I find myself keeping watch from the bridge
across the Callan: a snatch of hazel-wood
gives on to the open

range in which, once Jimmy McParland would turn
them out of the byre,
his cattle would cross-fade to Elmer Kelton's

stampeding herd
from *The Day the Cowboys Quit*, or *The Oklamydia Kid*,
or, hold on, something by Jack Schaefer.

After Cavafy and Elytis and Ritsos and Seferis
and Sikelianos and Vassilis Vassilikos come R. E. S. Wyatt's
The Inns and Outs of Cricket and *Bridge*

from A to Z by George S. Coffin: an 'insult to the heart'
was Livesey's diagnosis to the Squire
when Trelawney flew in from the Philippines

to visit S—— in Hazelden;
across the drumlins of Aughnacloy and Caledon and Keady
I myself flap like a little green heron.

Would that I might have put on hold
what must have sounded like a condemned man's last request
for a flagon of ale

while mine host was explaining how in some final over
he himself was the short slip
who caught that fiendish Gagoogly from *King Solomon's
    Mines.*

King Solomon's Mines; *The Sign of Four*; *The Lost World*; *Rob Roy*;
I would steady myself with Lancelot du Lac

as I grasped with both hands
my sword in the stone
(this was the rusted blade of a griffawn

embedded in a whitewashed wall);
I would grit my teeth and brace
myself against the plunge into Owl Creek.

I grit my teeth. I brace myself. It's 1:43
by the clock
on the V.C.R.: with one bound

Peyton Farquhar and I will break free and swim across
to Librium
with a leisurely crawl and flutter-kick.

An Occurrence at Owl Creek Bridge, The Ox-Bow Incident:
I've never been able to separate
'occurrence' from 'incident', 'owl' from 'ox';

in the first, I know, the narrative device
begins to – how shall I put it? – grate
a little, just as *un petit soupçon* of auteurism goes

a hell of a long way for myself, even,
despite my predilection for pushing out the boat,
never mind Pauline Kael.

The bridge. The barn. The all-too-familiar terrain.
I hear McParland's cattle low
as they plumb their murky bath

for a respite from their cattle-sorrow:
they're not to notice, taped to the trough, an aerial
and a battery-pack.

This looks suspiciously like a prize-fighter's arm
mounted behind glass. I drink
to Goneril's bland-

ishments and Cordelia's smart-ass '*Nada*'
from a tot of fusel oil.
My supper of cod-tongues and seal-

flipper pie repeats on me as I flipper through a Harp-
er and Row
first edition of cod-tongues and moose, medium rare,

washed down by the best beer in the U.S.,
the nonesuch 'Anchor Steam',
and remember one who did herself in *utcunque placuerit Deo.*

That must have been the year old Vladimir Vladimirovich
smoked kief all the way from *Alamein to mon Zem-
Zemblable* with *The Bride of Lammermoor*

and *Ada, or Ardor*:
that was the year, while Plath found solace in *The Bhagavad
Gita*, Jim Hawkins and I were putting in at Nassau.

While Jim and I were plundering the Spanish Main
from the Grenadines to Grand Cayman
she knew that even amidst fierce

flames she might yet plant centaury:
while Jim and I were sailing with Teach and Morgan
she was fixing the rubber ring

on a Mason jar;
even amidst fierce flames, the expiapiaratory rush
of poppies in July, October poppies.

To appease a *moon*-goddess, no? How to read that last line
in that last poem? Does it describe
the moon or the woman? I mean at the very end

of 'Edge'; 'Her blacks crackle and drag.'
Whose 'blacks'? Is it the woman on the funeral urn
or the moon? Are they both 'masturbating a glitter'?

I crouch with Jim in the apple-butt on the *Marie Celeste*
while my half-eaten pomeroy
shows me its teeth: a fine layer of talc

has bandaged my hands;
it's Mexico, 1918;
this arm belongs to the pugilist-poet, Arthur Cravan;

it's enshrined now on the wall
of the den between a plaster of Paris
cow's skull and a stuffed ortolan, or Carolina crake.

It's Mexico, 1918, and I'm leaning out over the strake
with the inconsolable Myrna Loy,
whose poet-pugilist's

yawl
has almost certainly sunk like a stone:
'*J'y avais trouvé une combinaison idéal et idyllique* –

mon Artilutteur Ecrivain';
the label on the rake reads 'Pierce';
I'm thinking of those who have died by their own hands.

The scent of new-mown hay (it may be the scent of tonka)
pervades the 1848 edition of Clough's
The Bothie of Tofer-na-Fuosich: I know that ash-girt

well where a red
bullock with a stunningly white head
will again put its shoulder to the water like hardy Canute.

In a conventional sestina, that plaster of Paris skull
would almost certainly reveal the dent
where my da took a turf-spade to poleaxe

one of McParland's poley cows
that had run amuck on our spread,
bringing it to its knees by dint of a wallop so great

it must have ruptured a major vein,
such was the spout
of, like, blood that hit him full in the face.

When John L. Sullivan did for Jake Kilrain
in the seventy-fifth round, it was with such a blow
as left them both

utterly winded (note the caesura)
though no less so than Prince Peter and Mary O'Reilly
when they made the beast with two backs.

To find a pugilist-poet who'd tap his own prostate gland
for the piss-and-vinegar ink
in which he'd dash off a couple of 'sparrow-

songs', then jump headfirst into her fine how-d'-ye-do
heedless of whether she'd used a deo-
dorant, that was S——'s ideal:

after a twelve-hour day at Skadden, Arps
she wanted me to play Catullus
to her, like, Clodia; even now I savour her *arrière-*

goût of sweat and patchouli oil
and see, as she reaches for *The Interpretation of Dreams*,
that tattoo on her upper arm.

Even as I tug at the rusted blade of Excalibur
I can hear the gallant six hundred ride into the valley
and the Assyrian come down on the fold:

beyond the cattle-crush, beyond the piggery,
I fall headfirst with Peyton
Farquhar through doeskin and denim and dimity and damask.

Even now, after eight – almost ten – years, I savour
the whiff of patchouli oil and sweat:
from Avenue A, her view of Brooklyn Bridge

inspired her to 'kingdoms naked in the trembling heart –
Te Deum laudamus O Thou Hand of Fire';
and, should it happen

that He's lost his bit of Latin,
she would nevertheless have been understood by God,
to whom she appealed at every twist and turn.

'For your body is a temple,' my ma had said to Morholt,
'the temple of the Holy Ghost':
even now I see Morholt raise the visor of his pail

as he mulled this over;
the memory of an elk, or eland, struggling up a slope
must have been what darkened his dark mien.

Even now I savour her scent of jacaranda–jasmine:
even now I try to catch hold
of her as she steps from her diaphanous half-slip

with its lime-white gusset
and turns to me as if to ask, with the Lady Guinevere,
'What is the meaning of the Holy Grail?'

While my da studies the grain in the shaft of his rake
and I tug at the rusted blade of the loy
my ma ticks off a list

of seeds: Tohill, from *tuathal*,
meaning 'withershins' – with its regrettable overtones
of sun-worship – in our beloved Goidelic;

even as I head up a straggling caravan
of ragamuffins and rapparees
my rocking-horse's halter fast-forwards through my hands.

To the time I hunkered with Wyatt Earp and Wild Bill Hickok
on the ramparts of Troy
as Wild Bill tried to explain to Priam

how 'saboteur' derives from *sabot*, a clog:
to the time we drove ten thousand head from U-Cross
to Laramie with Jimi and Eric riding point.

Even as I lean forward to slacken Roland's martingale
the moonlit road from Ghent
to Aix

goes up in smoke and mirrors and marsh-gas
and a hound-spirit
can be heard all the way from the Great

Grimpen to Fitzroy Road; not since 1947
had a winter been so bad;
it seemed as though ice burned and was but the more ice.

If only Plath had been able to take up the slack
of the free rein
lent her so briefly by Ariel:

all I remember of that all-time low
of January, 1963, was a reprieve from Cicero
and the weekly hair-wash and bath.

That must have been the year they shut down Armagh
College: the Moy road was a rink;
all we had to eat was a bland

concoction of bread and milk known as 'panada'.
Though her mouth was smoother than oil,
the mouth of Christine Keel-

er, her end was sharp
as a two-edged sword, as the arrow
that flieth by day. Rich and rare

were the gems Dedalus
gave the Countess Irina, despite the *tempus edax rerum*
of that bloody-nosed 'Venus' clerk, Ovide'.

That was the year I stumbled on Publius Ovidius Naso
vying with Charlie Gunn in an elegiac distich:
the year Eric and Jimi rode picket

on the Chisholm
Trail and Mike Fink declaimed from his Advanced Reader
the salascient passages from *Amores*.

That was the year my da would find the larvae, or pupae,
of cabbage-whites on the acumen
of a leaf: my rocking-horse with the horse-hair mane

stopped in its tracks, giving me such a jar
I fell off, just as Utepandragun
himself was trotting by; 'How come you Fenians are so averse

to buying plants in Comber, that's loyal to the king,
instead of smuggling them in from Rush?
Buy stalwart plants from a stalwart Prod, albeit a dissenter.'

All I remember is how my da drew himself up like Popeye
as he gave a tight-lipped 'C'mon'
and by sheer might and main

stuffed Utepandragun into a spinach-jar:
'I'll have you know, you clouricane,
that I force

my own kale every Spring';
all I remember was the sudden rush
of blood from his nose, a rush of blood and snatters.

All I remember was a reprieve from '*seachain*
    droch-chómhluadar'
as she last rinsed my hair: she'd sung 'Eileen
Aroon'

or some such ditty and scrubbed and scrubbed
till the sink was full of dreck;
'Stay well away from those louts and layabouts at the
    loanin'-end.'

Was it not now time, they urged, to levy the weregild, the *éiric*,
on the seed and breed of that scum-bag, Mountjoy,
that semioticonoclast

who took it upon himself to smash Shane O'Neill's
coronation-stone
on the chalky slopes of Tullahogue?

Was it not now time for the Irish to break the graven
image of a Queen whose very blotting-paper
was black, black with so much blood on her hands?

Like a little green heron, or 'fly-up-the-creek',
I flap above Carrickmore and Pomeroy
with volume one of Burton's translation of *The Lusiads*:

'One for all,'
I hear a cry go up, 'and all for one,'
followed by '*S'é tuar oilc*

an t-éan sin, agus leabhar in a chroibhín';
that was the year I did battle with Sir Bors
for Iseult the Fair (not Iseult of the White Hands).

That was the year Deirdre watched Jimi cut the tongue
from a Hereford calf
while a raven drank its blood: she pulled on her cigarette;

'Is there no man with snow-white skin and cheeks red
as blood and a crow-black head
in all of Ulster and Munster and Leinster and Connaught?'

That was the year my ma gave me a copy of Eleanor Knott's
Irish Classical Poetry and I first got my tongue
around *An Craoibhín Aoibhinn* (Douglas Hyde):

I was much less interested in a yellowed copy of *An
        Claidheamh
Soluis* than *Tschiffley's Ride* or *The Red
Rover* or *A Connecticut Yankee in King Arthur's Court*.

That was the year of such frost and snow and burning ice
I was kept home from school
for almost two weeks:

the year the stork or some such great
bird was blown off course and loitered with intent
on the west spire of the twin-spired

Armagh cathedral; my ragamuffins
and rapparees, meanwhile, were champing at the bit
for the slightest *belli casus.*

Surely the time had come for the Irish to strike back
at the *Defensor Fidei*, the peerless Oriana,
by whose command Patrick Pearse and The O'Rahilly

were put up against a wall? Was that not a *casus belli*?
Put up against a wall, like this ortolan, or sora,
and shot at the whim of Elizabloodybeth.

The day S—— came back with the arrow
through a heart tattooed on her upper arm, it made me think
of the fleur-de-lys

on Milady's shoulder (not Milady Clark, who helped
        the U.D.A.
run a shipment of Aramis
into Kilkeel

but Milady *Clarik*, whose great-great-grandfather led
        the I.R.B.
invasion of Canada, the one who helped foil
the plot in which the courier

was none other than herself, her): she shrugs off her taffeta
wither-band and begs me to, like, rim
her for Land's sakes; instead of 'Lord', she says 'Land'.

Throughout all this she wears some kind of ski-hood or -mask
(what she terms her 'clobber-clobber'):
as the peyote-button

begins to take effect, she shrugs off her *feileadh
beag* and turns up Jean Michel Jarre's loathsome
        hocus-pokery;
Jean Michel Jarre or the loathsome Mike Oldfield.

'Wither' as in 'widdersinnes', meaning to turn
against the sun: she ticks off 'carrots', 'parsnips', 'swedes'
while I suffer

the tortures of the damned, imagining myself a Shackleton
frozen by fire;
'parsnips', 'swedes'; for, unless I manage to purge

myself of concupiscent thoughts and keep a weather-eye open
for the least occasion of sin, the Gates
of Glory will be barred to me, not being pure of heart.

While I skellied up and down the ward in the South Tyrone
Hospital she toyed with her cream of wheat
with its scallop-shell of Chivers:

of all the peers and Paladins
who'd been entangled in a coil of barbed-wire
at the battle of Bearosche,

Gawain mourned none more than his war-dobbins
Mancho and Gato
and Ingliart 'With the Short Ears', his dear Ingliart.

Mother o'mine. Mother o'mine. That silver-haired mother
    o'mine.
With what conviction did she hold
that a single lapse – from *lapsus*, a slip

or stumble – would have a body cast
into the outer dark. Dost thou know Dover?
The foul fiend haunts poor Tom in the voice of a nightingale.

Since every woman was at heart a rake
and the purest heart itself marred by some base alloy
and whosoever looketh on a woman to lust

after her would go the way of Charles Stewart Parnell,
'*Ná bac*,' she would intone,
'*ná bac leis an duilleog*

rua ar an craoibhín
aoibhinn álainn óg,' and, rummaging in her purse,
'For Satan finds some mischief still for idle hands.'

'May your word be as good as or better than your bond,'
my ma was saying to Queequeg
as she made a sign of the Cross

over the tray:
when would we Irish find our *lán glaice*
of nutmeg to sweeten our barium?

.

That was the year there blew such an almighty gale
it not only bent
our poplars out of shape but downed one of the few oaks

left standing after Cill Cais.
We heated a saucepan of milk on a spirit-
stove and dreamed of the day when we Irish might grate

a little nutmeg over our oatmeal. The reek of paraffin.
When might we sweeten our stirabout
with *un petit soupçon* of nutmeg or some such spice?

'*Non,*' I heard from the depths of the barn, '*Je ne regrette rien*':
Edith Piaf, I thought, but lo
and behold, if it wasn't Sir Reginald Front-de-Boeuf

and Ben Gunn, fresh from the battle of Zara;
Ben had armed himself with a hurley
and both *Wisden's Cricketer's* and *Old Moore's* almanacs.

Now that the whole country, Ben volunteered, was going
     to rack,
faraoir, to rack and ruin,
now that the bird had perched for a week on the west oriel,

was it not now time to take down the hogweed blow-
gun that had stood me in such good stead against Assyria?
(Hogweed was perfect, having no pith.)

It might have been hogweed, or horehound, perhaps even
        arum,
that would inundate this rinky-dink
bit of land

on which a mushroom-mogul has since built a hacienda:
our own *Defensor Fidei* is somewhat reminiscent of Olyve Oyl
as she continues to reel

off in her own loopy version of R.P.
'parsnips', 'swedes', and, I guess, 'vegetable marrow';
hers is a sensibility so rare

that I'll first know Apuleius
as the author of *The Golden Beam*;
'It should be *Fidei Defensor*, by the way, not *Defensor Fidei*.'

That must have been the year I stood by the wheel-barrow
with Davy Crockett and Mike Fink
to recite the Angelus:

we followed that with a rousing medley of 'Me and Me Da',
'Believe Me If All Those Endearing Young Charms',
'Do Ye Ken John Peel?'

and, to round it off, 'An Arab's
Farewell to His Steed'; Mike opened a packet wrapped
        in foil
and shook out on to a piece of Carrara

a kilo of black powder he then divvied
up into charges of exactly eleven drachms,
admirable for medium-sized game – sable antelope or eland.

Mike was holding forth to Virgil Earp on how Dido and
    Aeneas
sometimes got so close you couldn't tell which
was which and that was how they 'begat'

in olden days, though things had changed some,
mostly for the worse: Mike fancied himself as an orator;
'*O tempora!*' he would extemporise, '*O mores!*'

'*Sé mo mhíle brón,*' Ben wept, '*tu bheith sínte fuar i measc
na dtom*' as Rashleigh and Caleb, er,
Balderstone gave his brother, Charlie, a sup of poteen:

that was the year Armagh would lose to Offaly
and my band of buccaneers and buckaroos
would weep openly over the corpse of poor, poor, poor
    Foulata.

That must have been the year S—— and the mighty Umbopa
were playing mah-jong or backgammon
with Allan Quatermain

and myself when a fey curled out of the jar
and spoke to her: this, of course, was the Fata Morgana,
the Great Queen of the Fairies,

who recognized Umbopa as her once and future king;
it looked as if S—— was still having a cocaine-rush
after almost a month in the rehab centre.

That was the year Mike Fink – 'half-horse, half-alligator' –
appealed to *The First Oration against Catiline*
as he mused on the times that were in it when a Grey Heron

or a Great Crested Grebe
or, more likely than not, a White Stork
could have the country debating what evil it might portend.

The blow-gun was still sleek with Wright's Coal Tar:
there was a hair-line
crack from the fall I took when an Assyrian

ran me through; we'd held the bridge against Sennacherib,
of course, despite his trick
of torching the barn, which was where Aladdin met his end.

That was the year, after the Caliph of Baghdad, Haroun,
had forced him to eat his own weight
in emeralds and sapphires,

the doughty Aladdin
had a Michelin-man spare tyre:
it was Aladdin who gave Prince Peter the salamander brooch

Prince Peter gave the Countess Irina, whereupon
Popeye exclaimed to Quatermain and Curtis and
        Captain Good,
'Somebody here is gonna get hurt.'

The bridge. The barn. The all-too-familiar seal-flipper terrine
with the hint of seaweed
(carrageen? samphire?)

that lent it the texture of gelatin.
Again and again S—— turns up 'The Unforgettable Fire'
and shrugs off her halter of buckram or barege

and holds herself open;
my ma hands me the carbon-slip; 'But to the girdle do
    the gods,'
she repeats, 'but to the girdle do the gods inherit.'

That night I dreamed – *Te Deum laudamus, In Nomine
    Domini –*
that the hornless doe, *an eilit
mhaol,* came to me as a slip

of a girl and laid her exquisite
flank beside me under the covers
and offered me her breast, her breast *chomh bán le haol.*

'How much longer', she cajoled, 'must we rant and rail
against the ermine
yoke of the House of Hanover?

When might the roots of Freedom take hold?
For how much longer must we cosset
Freedom's green shoot and Freedom's little green slip?'

The following morning I got up at the scrake
of dawn and struggled into my corduroy
breeks and packed the blow-gun and the cobbler's last

and awl
into the trunk of the two-tone
(pink and cream) '62 Cadillac

with a gryphon
rampant on its hood, switched on the windshield wipers
and sped away, look, no hands.

Little did I know, as I began to rake
across the snowy yard, how short-lived would be my joy:
for I had unwittingly entered the lists

against John Ridd and Jack McCall
and Rashleigh Osbaldistone
and other villains of that ilk;

this is not to speak of Agravain
and his little platoon of pirries
and djinns; I mean the dastardly 'Agravain of the Hard
      Hand'.

Little did I know that Agravain was weighing his
    knobkerrieknout:
not even the tongue
of fire that will-o'-the-wisped above my head

would save me; 'I'd as lief,'
Agravain was muttering, 'I'd as lief you'd stay and help
    me redd
up after the bluestone barrels are scoured.'

Little did I think that S—— would turn to me one night:
'The only Saracen I know's a Saracen tank
with a lion rampant on its hood;

from Aghalane to Artigarvan to Articlave
the Erne and the Foyle and the Bann must run red';
that must have been the year Twala's troops were massacred.

Now I took the little awl I'd used with such consummate skill
to scuttle *The Golden Vanitee*
and picked the locks

on the old suitcase
in which was hidden the two-page spread
from *The News of the World*: after stopping by the cattle-grid

to pick up Laudine and Yvain
I smiled as I thought of the awl (was it a brace and bit?)
wrapped in a photo of Mandy Rice Davies.

The two-tone Cadillac's engine-block was a vice
lapped in a coil
of barbed wire and wedged between an apple-box

and a packing-crate:
as I crossed the bridge, I was so intent
on Freedom's green slip and Freedom's green sprout

her '*Ná bac leis an craoibhín aoibhinn*'
and 'Stay clear of those louts and layabouts'
were quite lost on me; I promptly stepped on the gas.

'O come ye back,' I heard her sing, 'O come ye back
to Erin':
I was somewhat more exercised by the fact that my yourali

supply was running so low
I might well have to spend my last cruzeiro
on an ounce of civet, or resort to my precious *Bufo bufo*.

The magical toad entrusted to me by Francisco Pizarro
might still be good against this bird that continued to prink
itself, alas,

even as we left Sitanda's
kraal and struck out, God between us and all harm,
for the deep north: that was the year Jack McCall would deal

the dead man's hand to Earp,
the year Captain Good was obliged to shave in inco-oil
and S—— got hooked on 'curare';

the year Scragga and Infadoos
joined Quatermain in reciting 'The Jackdaw of Rheims'
as we plunged deeper into Kukuanaland.

Only yesterday, as I shlepped out to Newark on the PATH
whom should I spot but two Japanese guys wearing
    fanny-packs:
I recognized them as 'Basho' and 'Sora'

from Avenue A; I knew by the tags on their mule-train
that they were just getting back from the Lowlands Low;
'Tooralooraloora,' Basho gave me a stupid grin,
    'tooralooralay.'

'Tirra lirra,' S—— sang when we were stopped by the 'fuzz'
as she drove back to school:
she was reading, it seemed, as deeply into Maalox

as Malebranche, Rennies as René Descartes:
I helped her move into a 'pad', as she styled her apartment,
in which Herrick's *Hesperides* and a can of Sprite

and Duchamp's 'The Bride Stripped Bare by Her Bachelors,
        Even'
all said one thing – 'I masturbate';
she was writing now on *Ulster: From C. S. Lewis to C. S. Gas.*

'Tirra lirra lirra,' was what she sang to Umslopogaas
and myself to, like, break the ice
when we first went to see her in detox:

an albino ginko, or some such sport;
she was now deeply into Lloyd Cole
and Julio Cortázar and, *Dios me libre*, Fuentes;

Lloyd 'King' Cole, she'd dubbed him; Warren Zevon;
as for U2's Edge, his 'Bad'
put him up there with Jimi and Eric, a 'Guitar Great'.

Five days north of Sitanda's kraal we were joined by Sigurd,
his twin cousins, Hrut and Knut,
and Lieutenant Henry Ark, also known as Eric the Red:

it was Eric who cut us each a strip of biltong
from the shield carried by his son, Leif;
Leif Ericson's shield was covered with chlordiazepoxide.

'How dare you,' began Milady Clarik, 'how dare you
      desecrate
the memory of Connolly and Clarke and Ceannt':
she brandished *The Little Red*

Book of Mao Tse-Tung;
'How dare you blather on about the Caliph
of Baghdad when you should strike while the iron's hot.'

'Surely,' S—— chimed in, 'surely the time is at hand
for the Hatfields and McCoys
to recognize their common bond?' (It was Milady *Clark*

who'd given her a copy of Ian Adamson's *The Cruthin*,
of which she'd bought a thousand tonnes
for 'intellectual ballast'.)

Together they'd entered into dialogue
with the first mate of a ship registered in Valparaiso
who had 'connections' in the Transvaal.

Ben Gunn would now gladly have red-hewed his right hand
for a piece of mouse-trap cheese, when the fairy Terdelaschoye
rustled up some *Caprice des Dieux*: so it was that Erec

and Enid and I hoisted the main-sail (complete with raven)
and hung the lodestone
by an elast-

ic band; *Caprice*, for Land's sake, from the 'goat-like'
caprioles and capers
of those Athenian galleys with their tu-whit-tutelary owls.

Only moments later, I was bending over to tie a slip-
knot when I looked up suddenly and the rough tree rail
had been superseded by the coast

of Africa; it struck me then that the limpet-mine
in the *Hispaniola*'s hold
had been planted there by the pesky Pedro Navarro.

That must have been from our last trip up the Guadalquivir:
we'd given the Athenian galleys the slip
and put in at Seville rather than try to hold

our course for Dover, its cliffs *chomh bán le haol,*
with our cargo of calomel (or calamine);
the Guadalquivir had been our Rubicon; the die was cast.

To make matters worse, Ben reported that he'd just heard
the unmistakable tu-whit
tu-whoo of the *gubernaculum* in the stern

of a Roman galley. We were getting ready to open
fire
on anything that moved when '*Vamos, muchachos, vamos
a ver*'

came out of nowhere, followed by a barge
with a triangular sail – a jib, to be precise – cut
from a single piece of lateen.

From the cut of their jib we took the crew for a horde
of Cruthin dyed with woad:
it hadn't occurred to us that we ourselves might turn

blue after a month in an open
boat; it transpired
these legionnaires had been set adrift by Septimius Severus

in 211 AD; we shared what was left of our porridge,
then joined them in a game of quoits
on the deck of the *Caledonia*.

Who should hove into view, with a boy-troop from St Enda's,
but Pearse himself: together with the gallioteers,
we went ashore and began the long trek

north from St Enda's kraal; when the tree-line
gave way to unfamiliar scrub
we knew we'd rounded not the Cape of Good Hope but
Cape Horn.

That was the year Mike Fink was a bouncer at 'The Bitter End'
on Bleecker Street: 'The times are out of kilter,'
he remarked to S——, eyeing the needle-tracks

on her arms; that was the year she would mainline
so much 'curare' they ran up two flags over her wing
    at Scripps.
(By 'curare', or 'yourali', she meant heroin.)

In view of these square red flags with square black centres
we turned back and fell to right away to gammon
the bow-sprit with baobab-

ropes and secure the cat's-head and the catharping
against the impending hurricane:
we'd already stowed the sails (fore-, mizzen- and main-)

and breamed the hull with burning furze
and touched up the figurehead – an angel carved by
      William Rush
from the sturdiest of mahoganies, the Australian jarrah.

All I remember is a thunder-cloud of dust across the veldt
(much like the rattle of Twala's Massagais
on shields) and Ben's 'Bejasus' and 'Begorrah'

as the dust-cloud engulfed the rigging of our clipper;
the courage, then, with which he and one or two other fellows
crawled from hatch to hatch to check the battens.

For a whole week we survived on pages torn from *Old Moore*
or *Wisden* and flavoured with star anise:
this was a trick Israel had picked up from a short-order

cook who'd sailed with Flint: Israel used a switch-
blade to peel and portion our last satsuma;
that year MacNeice and Frost and Plath all kicked the bucket.

The storm blew over, of course, and with the help of Arrow,
the first mate, and Nemo and Livesey, her shrinks,
we bundled S—— into the *Nautilus*

and set off for Grenada:
many's the old salt would swing from the yard-arm,
many's the sea-dog be keel-

hauled for failing to keep a sharp
lookout for Carthaginian hydrofoils;
after a month, she was transferred to the *Fighting Téméraire*

despite objections from the 'perfidious'
Trelawney having to do with her 'low self-esteem'
and her 'unhealthy interest' in Henri de Montherlant.

The next thing I knew, we were with Gonzalo Fernandez
        de Oviedo,
discombobulated by the clink
of mutinous men-at-arms,

upon a peak in Da-
rien: we'd been watching *The Irish in Us*
when the projector must have broken down during the third
        reel

and thrown me into a time-warp;
not only was S—— the dead spit of Olivia de Havilland
playing Liadan to my, like, Cuirithir

but (this chilled me to the marrow)
her face in the freeze-frame
was not unlike Maud Gonne's, swathed in a butterfly-net
        voile.

As we hunkered there in the projection-booth
the projector had gone, like, totally out of whack:
the freeze-frame of Maud Gonne from *Mise Eire*

had S—— strike up her all-too-familiar refrain;
'The women that I picked spoke sweet and low
and yet they all gave tongue, gave tongue right royally.'

Maud Gonne was explaining how 'San Graal' was a pun on
    '*Sang real*'
to 'Diana Vernon' and Constance Gore-Booth
when 'Blow me,' Popeye roared, 'blow

me down if I can't put my hand on the knapsack-
sprayer': Constance Gore-Booth was back from a trip to the
    Ukraine ·
with Milady Clarik, the aforementioned 'emissary'.

That was the year Yeats said to Plath, '*Mi casa es su casa*':
all the way from Drumcliff old 'Hound Voice'
could be heard; 'How much longer will the House of Saxe-

Coburg-Gotha try to break the spirit
of the Gael?
How much longer must we Irish vent

our spleen against their cold, their rook-delighting heaven?
When will we have at last put paid
to Milady's great-grandfather's foes?' (He meant
    'great-great'.)

So it was that every year for thirty years I'd bream
its clinkered hull, lest horehound or cuckoo-pint
or dandelion-clocks

should swamp my frail caïque:
for thirty years we ran before the wind from Monterey
to San Diego by way of Santa Cruz.

For thirty years I would serve on *The Golden Hind*:
thirty years, man and boy,
I sailed with Sir Humphrey Gilbert and Drake;

thirty years that led to the, like, raven-
stone
where Mary Queen of Scots herself lost

her head because she, too, was a 'Catlick';
thirty years before I understood what Lady Percy
and Hotspur meant by Milady's 'howl'.

It was thirty years till I reached back for the quiver
in which I'd hidden the carbon-slip
from Tohill's of the Moy: my hand found the hilt

of the dirk I confiscated from Israel;
the carbon-slip was gone; what with those 'persimmons'
and 'swedes', I'd been diverted from my quest.

In addition to missing the carbon-slip I was getting hard:
not since our family outing to White
and Boa Islands on Lower Lough Erne

(where a *Síle na gcíoch* held herself wide open)
had I been so mortified; it was then I noticed the
    command-wire
running all the way from behind a silver

birch
to the drinking-trough; that trough was my Skagerrak,
    my Kattegat,
its water a brilliant celadon.

As we neared Armagh, the Convent of the Sacred Heart
was awash in light: nor galloped less steadily Roland a whit
than when S—— ran

those five red lights in downtown New Haven:
    'George Oppen,'
she announced, 'there's a poet with fire
in his belly'; this was to the arresting 'officiffer'

who had her try to walk a straight line back to the Porsche;
after calling him 'the unvoiced "c" in Connecticut',
she gave our names as Cuirithir and Liadan.

Even now a larva was gnawing at her 'most secret and
      inviolate'
rose of Damascus:
as we neared Armagh, I could still hear her pecky, pecky,
      peckery

though it was drowned out by Mike's 'Cruise of the
      Calabar';
little did we know, as we galloped along the Folly,
that S—— had broken the seal on the little box marked
      Verboten.

As we neared Armagh, she'd dipped the tip of each little arrow
in the blood of an albino skink
or some such *lusus*

naturae: that must have been the year we ran cattle from
      Nevada
to Wyoming; the year, as we rode into Laramie
with Jimi and Eric and Shane (*the* Shane, not Shane O'Neill)

we heard from behind us, '*Manos arriba*';
'Parsnips,' I kept saying, 'parsnips and parzleval';
little did we know that a whole raree-

show led by Agravain and the Agraviados
had been on our case since S—— had dallied with Wolfram,
much to the chagrin – remember? – of Roland.

I seem to recall that she was even more into Barthes
than Wolfram von Eschenbach:
largely because of *Writing Degree Zero*

she now ran with a flock of post-Saussureans
who leapt about from 'high' to 'low'
like so many dyed-in-the-wool serows or oorials.

'Dyed-in-the-wool'; 'serow'; 'oorial': in the midst of chaos,
she would say, the word is a suspect device,
a Pandora's – that's it – *box*;

and she leaned over me the way a bow-sprit
(bow-sprit? martingale?)
leans over the water in search of a 'referent';

this last time I saw her, in New Haven,
she leaned over, so, and whispered, 'This darling bud,
this bud's for you,' then settled back on the packing-crate.

As we neared the Convent of the Sacred . . . of the Sacred
Heart, our way was blocked by a Knight
of the Red

Branch astride a skewbald mustn'tang:
I noticed, as he threw down his glove,
something familiar about his ski-mask, or his ski-hood.

'How dare you suggest that his "far-off, most secret,
and inviolate rose" is a cunt:
how dare you misread

his line about how they "all gave tongue";
how dare you suggest that *Il Duce* of Drumcliff
meant that "Diana Vernon" and Maud Gonne gave
    good head.'

Though his mustn'tang stood at a good twelve hands
the Knight and his armour weighed at least four hundred
      pounds troy
so that when I tapped him with the rake

he succumbed as readily as the boar-king, Ysgithrwyn,
to Arthur's glaive: '*Níl aon tinteán,*'
S—— was confiding to Livesey and Zorro, the analysts,

'*mar do thinteán féin*'; she'd dreamed that a huge deelawg
or earwig or, as she preferred, a '*perce-
oreille*', had caught her in its pincers near some ash-girt well.

As we finally reached Armagh things were badly out of hand:
it was now too late to seek and destroy
that ominous bird of yore: not since the bold Theodoric

hopped the twig in Ravenna
had we witnessed such pomp and circumstance;
even Theodoric was outclassed

by this, the funeral cortège of Cardinal Dalton (Dalton
    or Logue?)
who'd taken a turn – surprise, surprise –
the very day and hour he looked upon that fearsome fowl of ill.

It was now too late for Erec to pull out of Enid
while she masturbated her clitoris
and S—— and I, like, outparamoured the Turk

in the next room: the scent of Vaseline;
her fondness for the crop;
the *arrière-goût* of patchouli oil and urine.

There was nothing for it, after Ben had dispatched the sentry
with a tap of his trusty *camán*,
but to load the breech of the drain-pipe

with Richardson's Two-Sward: just then I heard the Lorelei
    sing
to an American
bomber sweeping the Rhine and the Main;

even now I smell the phosphorus
when I lit the fuse – the terminal spike of a bulrush
I'd kept tinder-dry in a sealed jam-jar.

For the time was now ripe, S—— had vowed, to 'make
          a *Sendero*
Luminoso of our *Camino*
Real': along with the tattoo, she'd taken to wearing a labiaba-

ring
featuring a salamander, a salamander being the paragon
of constancy; it was twenty years to the month the water-main

froze
on Fitzroy Road and the *T.L.S.* had given the bum's rush
to *The Bell Jar*.

It was now too late, as I crouched with Cuchulainn and Emer,
to feel anything much but nausea
as again and again S—— cast about for an artery:

I'd not be surprised if this were some kind of time-switch
taped to the trough, that the click of a zoom;
such nausea (from *navis*, a ship) as I'd not felt since
　　the *Pequod*.

For I'd not be surprised if this were a video
camera giving me a nod and a wink
from the blue corner, if it were hooked up not to an alarm

but the TV, that I myself am laid out on a da-
venport in this 'supremely Joycean object, a nautilus
of memory jammed next to memory', that I'll shortly reel

with Schwitters and Arp
through our *Kathedrale des erotischen Elends*
while the bobolink, rare

bird that she is, feeds on the corpse from *Run of the Arrow*,
leaving off only fitfully to scream
in Gaelakota, '*Ná bac leis. Ná bac leis, a Phóil.*'

This is some goddess of battle, Macha or Badhbh,
whose 'Ná bac
leis, a Phóil' translates as 'Take heed, sirrah:

you must refrain ·
from peeking down my dress, though it's cut so low
you may see my aureoles.'

This is Badhbh, or Macha, or Morrigan – the greatest of great
queens – whose cackle-caws
translate as *tempus rerum edax*:

'Where on earth,' she croaks, 'where on earth have you spent
the past half-hour?' 'I've just lit the fuse
on a cannon,' I begin, sticking the glowing coal

in my pocket. 'What in under heaven
did we do to deserve you, taking off like that, in a U-boat,
when you knew rightly the spuds needed sprayed?'

At first it seemed that the louts and layabouts at the cross
might have stolen the prime
from my touch-hole and sold it to, like, Henry of Ballantrae

and the acumen, or point,
of the bulrush had been lost on the powder-keg;
the deelawg was not so much an earwig, I suspect, as a clock.

'Take Neruda,' S—— volunteered, 'a poet who dirtied his
	hands
like a *bona fide* minstrel boy
gone to the wars in Tacna-Arica:

if he's not to refine
himself out of existence, if he's not to end up on methadone,
the poet who wants to last

must immerse himself in Tacna-Arica and Talca';
the larva, meanwhile, of *Pieris
brassicae* was working through kale and cauliflower *et al*.

I crouch with Schwitters and Arp in the house in Hanover
that stands like a ship on the slips
when, lo and behold,

the sky opens and it begins to hail
codeine and amyl nitrate and sulphides and amphetamines
and Mike Oldfield and Jean Michel Jarre cassettes.

'Vengeance is mine,' proclaimed my armchair anarchist
to the pesky Ramon Navarro,
'mine and mine

alone'; even now the hounds were straining at their slips
as the hornless doe, *an eilit mhaol,*
stumbles out of *A Witness Tree*; New York, 1942;
    Henry Holt.

Again and again I flap through Aughnacloy and Caledon:
Tray, Blanche and Sweet-
heart

are dogs that must to kennel while Milady's brach
doth stand by the fire
with the red-eyed towhee, turn, turn, turn;

Don Junipero, meanwhile, weighed down with silver,
finds his way back from codeine to *kodeia*,
the 'poppy-head' much loved by the towhee, or marsh robin.

Again and again the maudlin towhee flaps over Bonn or
    Baden-Baden
like an American bomber on a night-flight
along the Rhine valley

as Salah-ed-din holds the larva (from *larva*, a ghost or mask)
in forceps, maybe, or catticallipillers;
he holds it close to his chest like Hickok's last hand in
    baccarat.

S—— would detect the mating-call of Fine Gael or Fianna Fáil
in that red-eyed chewink's
'Fadó, fadó':

'Ní fiú liom sin,' she would say, 'Ní fiú sin dada';
now her tattoo of a heart and arrow
was all but crowded out by those cochineal

sores not unlike those of herp-
es or chlamydia; I should have known this was no boxer's arm,
faraoir, faraoir,

about to land
a haymaker, but a prize carp, or a prize bream,
or the dreaded Dracunculus.

That last time I stood by her side, like some latterday Uriel,
she sang the praises of 'The Shining Path'
while she cut a line of coke with a line of Sweet 'n Low:

then she lay down by the tracks
and waited for the train
that would carry Deirdre and Naoise back to Assaroe.

All I remember is a lonesome tu-whit tu-whoo from the crate
and her bitter, 'What have *you* done for the cause?
You're just another Sir Pertinax

MacSycophant,
brown-nosing some Brit who's sitting on your face
and thinking it's, like, really cool.'

She brandished a bottle of Evian;
'Thing is, *a Phóil*, your head's so far up your own fat butt
you've pretty much disappeared.'

Ten years after Plath set the napkin under her head
I got out from under S——'s cheese-cloth skirt
where what I'd taken for a nutmeg-clove

tasted now of monk's-hood, or aconite:
'*No tengo*,' the salamander fumed, '*no tengo
mas que darte*'; and I saw red, red, red, red, red.

'Nevermore,' my ma chipped in, 'will the soul clap its hands
for sheer joy
as it did for Yeats and William Blake:

the legacy of Arthur Griffin'
(she meant Griff*ith*) 'and Emmet and Wolfe Tone
is lost, completely lost

on our loanin'-end ideologues,
while the legacy of Connolly and, God help us, Pearse
is the latest pell-mell in Pall Mall.'

Again and again I'm about to touch down by the
      pebble-dashed wall
(by way of Keady and Aughnacloy)
when it hits me that the house has changed hands:

the original of that salamander dalk
such as might have graced the lime-white throat of Etain
was recovered near Dunluce or Dunseverick

or wherever the *Girona* was Dunsevericked or Dunluced;
in the 1931 *Connecticut Yankee* Myrna Loy appears
as Morgan the Fay; my ma is now in the arms of
      Sister Morphine.

'For every Neruda,' mused the bloody-nosed Countess Irina,
'must have his, like, Allende':
with that she handed back to Prince Peter the scarab

for which he'd paid a thousand guilders
and went back to cutting the line of coke with the line
of dalk, from the Anglo-Saxon *dalc* or *dolc*, a brooch or torc.

In due course Prince Peter sent a tape of Jean Michel Jarre's
Equinoxe to the commune
in Portland and, though it was returned to sender,

he realized from the thuriferous
scent that S—— must have gone off to Portland, Oregon,
with Yogi Bear and Boo-Boo

rather than Portland, like, Maine;
he realized, moreover, that she'd scrawled 'RUSH'
on the packet, which now contained a carbon-slip and a ring.

A carbon-slip? A ring? As he slipped it back in the packet
the salamander's double-edged 'nothing more'
cut him in two like a scim-

itar and he crouched with Naoise
after the limestone slab had crushed both Deirdre and
    the witch,
that being it, as they say, for the old Gagoolic order.

The ring? The carbon-slip? It's 1:49 and the video's
now so wildly out of synch
there's no telling *Some Experiences of an Irish R.M.*

from *The Shaggy D.A.*:
in Frost's great poem, 'The Most of It', the 'talus'
refers not to a heel,

of course, but the cliff-face or scarp
up which his moose or eland
will so memorably rear – 'rare',

my da would have said – while the Cathedral of Ero-
tic Misery, like that of Rheims,
will soon be awash in blood, in blood and sacred oil.

For that bobolink was no more your common oriole
than was Barton Booth
your common bletherskite: his 'Blow,

winds, and crack
your cheeks! Spit, fire! Spout, rain!'
would cut through the cackle like the mark of Zorro.

I crouch with Jim and Ben and our black-cloaked desperado
in a high-sided, two-wheeled *carreta*
full of hides and tallow and what must be retted flax.

Chlamydia: from *chlamys*, a cloak or cowl;
the filthy mantle on the gas;
again she renews her vows

to the moon-goddess; again she turns on the oven;
again the Agraviados begin to lay about
them while their Captain cries, 'Avaunt ye curs, avaunt.'

Now Father McEntaggart flings off his black, black cloak:
'This, Brigid, is a cross
you must bear with fortitude': as he gives her a cake

from the pyx (the mini-ciborium)
the dogs, for some reason, stand at point;
she calls to them in turn, to Sweetheart, Blanche and Tray.

Through Caledon and Aughnacloy the little dogs and all
are hard on my heels: they're led by that no good hobbledehoy
by the name of Israel Hands

who again clambers out of an Edmund Dulac
half-tone
to launch his Blitzkrieg

on Jim and myself; again the *Hispaniola* will take a sudden list
and Israel's dirk-blade pierce
my shoulder-muscle and its tendons be rent and riven.

The bridge. The barn. Again and again I stand aghast
as I contemplate what never
again will be mine:

'Look on her. Look, her lips.
Listen to her *râle*
where ovarian cancer takes her in its strangle-hold.'

Sharp was her end as the scimitar of Salah-ed-din
with which he cut through . . . what?
A cushion? A pillow? That was the year Richard the Lionheart

floated barrage-
balloons all along the coast between Jaffa and Tyre;
the year Lionheart smote an iron

bar with such force as so far,
so good, while Salah-ed-din, ever the more delicate,
sliced through the right Fallopian.

And there lay the mare – after they sliced her open –
there lay the mare with her nostril all wide
while Badhbh, daughter of Cailidin,

cried out on her behalf, 'Whosoever
looketh upon a woman with carnal desire
as after the water brooks panteth the hart . . .'

'Ovarian,' did I write? Uterine.
Salah-ed-din would slice through in his De Havilland
    Mosquito.
'American,' did I write? British.

All I remember was the linen cloth, at once primped and
    puckery,
where her chin rested on the patten:
'I'm living in Drumlister,' she says, 'in clabber

to the knee'; that was the year Salah-ed-din took the field
at Acre and with the fine edge of his damask
blade lopped off the right arm of Caius Mucius Scaevola.

Salah-ed-din would now seem poised to run a foil
through the weakest link
in the moon-suit wrought by some vidua

or whidah
bird while the scald crow,
Badhbh, latches on to the wheals

on the broken body of Tarp-
eia on whom, alas, the Sabines dumped their arms
as decisively as a bomber sweeping the Ruhr

would dump on Childe Roland:
an ampoule of Lustau's port, another of Bristol Cream,
are jittery in their tantalus.

I crouch with Schwitters and Arp, with Tristan Tzara,
as the Lorelei
lillibullabies from the Rhine,

thus affording the bomber a clear flight-path
through the ack-ack, or flak,
by which a dozen Spitfires have already been laid low.

Only yesterday I heard the cry go up, '*Vene sancti Spiritu,*'
as our old crate
overshot the runway at Halifax,

Nova Scotia: again I heard Oglalagalagool's
cackackle-Kiowas
as blood gushed from every orifice;

an ampoule of Lustau's port; a photograph of Godfrey Evans
who used to keep wicket – perhaps even went to bat –
for the noble and true-hearted Kent.

And here lies the mare with her nostril all wide and red
as I sit with her head
'twixt my knees: still appealing to Wakantanka,

our friends the Sioux, as they excoriate
Michael Jackson; all that's left of him is his top note;
'Why should a dog, a horse, a rat have life?'

There's not even an arm, not an arm left of Arthur Cravan,
for whom the disconsolate Mina Loy
would howl, howl, howl

when he upped and went: after the bomb-blast
has rained down clay and stones
and arms and legs and feet and hands

I should, I guess, help Mina rake
over these misrememberings for some sign of Ambrose Bierce,
maybe, if not her own Quetzalcoatliac.

Again and again, I hover in Bierce's 'good, kind dark'
while a young R.N.
hooks an I.V. into her arm: it must have been 'The Bottom
   Line'

rather than 'The Bitter End':
that must have been the year S—— wrote 'Helter-skelter'
in her own blood on the wall; she'd hidden a razor in her
   scrubs.

All would be swept away: the T'ang chamber-pot and
    the Ming;
again and again I wedge my trusty Camoëns
in the barn-door to keep it ajar

lest Agravyn à la Dure Mayn
mistake me for Ladon or some apple-butt dragon
and come after me; even now I hear his shuffle-saunter

through the yard, his slapping the bib
of his overalls; even now he stops by the cattle-crush
from which the peers and paladins would set out on their
    forays.

Again and again I look out over the bridge where Deirdre
dashed her head against the 'Begad,
I'll teach him not to mitch

when the spuds need spraying'; again and again the cruel Emir
stops with the High King, Connor MacNessa,
at the barn-door; again and again they cry out,
    'Open, Sesame.'

The bridge, the barn: the tongue of a boot once lus-
trous with mink-
oil;

a rocking-horse's hoof; the family tree from *Ada*;
all swept away in the bob and
wheel

of the sonata for flute and harp,
the wild harp hanged on a willow by Wolfgang Amadeo;
again and again Lear enters with a rare

and radiant maiden in his arms
who might at any moment fret and fream,
'I am the arrow that flieth by day. I am the arrow.'

In a conventional tornada, the strains of her 'Che sera, sera'
or 'The Harp That Once' would transport me back
to a bath resplendent with yarrow

(it's really a sink set on breeze- or cinder-blocks):
then I might be delivered
from the rail's monotonous 'alack, alack';

in a conventional envoy, her voice would be ever
soft, gentle and low
and the chrism of milfoil might over-

flow
as the great wheel
came full circle; here a bittern's bibulous 'Orinochone O'

is counterpointed only by that corncrake, by the gulder-gowl
of a nightjar, I guess, above the open-cast mines,
by a quail's

indecipherable code; of the great cog-wheel, all that remains
is a rush of air – a wing-beat,
more like – past my head; even as I try to regain

my equilibrium, there's no more relief, no more respite
than when I scurried, click, down McParland's lane
with my arms crossed, click, under my armpits;

I can no more read between the lines
of the quail's 'Wet-my-lips' or his 'Quick, quick'
than get to grips with Friedrich Hölderlin

or that phrase in Vallejo having to do with the 'ache'
in his forearms; on the freshly-laid asphalt
a freshly-peeled willow-switch, or baton, shows a vivid mosaic

of gold on a black field, while over the fields
of buckwheat it's harder and harder to pin down a gowk's
poopookarian *ignis fatuus*;

though it slips, the great cog,
there's something about the quail's 'Wet-my-foot'
and the sink full of hart's-tongue, borage and common kedlock

that I've either forgotten or disavowed;
it has to do with a trireme, laden with ravensara,
that was lost with all hands between Ireland and Montevideo.

Printed in the United States
1024800002B